SandCastle™

Animal Sounds

Bees BUZZ!

Pam Scheunemann

Consulting Editor, Diane Craig, M.A./Reading Specialist

ABDO
Publishing Company

Published by ABDO Publishing Company, 8000 West 78th Street, Edina, Minnesota 55439.

Copyright © 2009 by Abdo Consulting Group, Inc. International copyrights reserved in all countries.

No part of this book may be reproduced in any form without written permission from the publisher.
SandCastle™ is a trademark and logo of ABDO Publishing Company.

Printed in the United States.

Editor: Katherine Hengel
Content Developer: Nancy Tuminelly
Cover and Interior Design and Production: Oona Gaarder-Juntti, Mighty Media
Photo Credits: AbleStock, ShutterStock

Library of Congress Cataloging-in-Publication Data

Scheunemann, Pam, 1955-
  Bees buzz! / Pam Scheunemann.
    p. cm. -- (Animal sounds)
  ISBN 978-1-60453-567-9
  1. Bees--Juvenile literature. I. Title.
  QL565.2.S34 2009
  595.79'9--dc22
                              2008033917

Bees have wings to fly.

Honeybees have two pairs of wings. They can fly up to 15 miles per hour (24 km/h)!

You can hear them buzzing by.

A bee's wings flap about 11,000 times a minute. That's what makes the buzzing sound.

They buzz as they fly high and low.

Bees gather food every day.
They travel up to six miles
(10 km) per trip.

Bees look for where the flowers grow.

Flowers make a sugary liquid called nectar. The bees need the nectar to make honey.

Bees take nectar
from different flowers.

Bees have tiny hairs all over their bodies. The pollen found on flowers sticks to these hairs.

They fly around for many hours.

In just one trip, a bee will collect nectar from more than 1,000 flowers.

Bees return when they get the chance. If they found nectar, they will dance!

When a bee finds a good nectar source, it returns to the hive and does a special dance. Its dance tells the other bees where the nectar is.

The nectar they find is very sweet.

Unlike humans, bees can see ultraviolet light. Ultraviolet light shows bees where the nectar is in the flower.

It becomes the honey we like to eat!

Nectar from different flowers makes honey taste different. There are over 300 unique flavors of honey in the United States.

Each bee has a special job to do.

Young worker bees take care of the babies and build and repair the hive. Only the oldest worker bees search for nectar.

I like the buzzing of bees, don't you?

The buzzing sound of a beehive is caused by worker bees beating their wings inside the hive. This is how bees control the temperature in the hive.

Glossary

flap (p. 4) – to move up and down or back and forth.

flavor (p. 18) – the taste of something.

hive (pp. 15, 20, 23) – a nest or container in which a colony of bees lives.

imitate (p. 24) – to copy or mimic someone or something.

pollen (p. 11) – the tiny yellow grains produced by flowers.

source (p. 15) – the point where something comes from or begins.

temperature (p. 23) – a measure of how hot or cold something is.

ultraviolet light (p. 17) – a type of light that cannot be seen with the human eye.

unique (p. 18) – the only one of its kind.

Animal Sounds Around the World

Bees sound the same no matter where they live. But the way that humans imitate them depends on what language they speak. Here are some examples of how people around the world make bee sounds:

English – buzz   **French** – bzzz
German – summ   **Greek** – zoum
Japanese – boon boon   **Spanish** – bzzz